MESSAGE OF FATIMA

In the life of the Church
and teaching of the Popes

by
Timothy Tindal-Robertson

*All booklets are published thanks to the
generous support of the members of the
Catholic Truth Society*

CATHOLIC TRUTH SOCIETY
PUBLISHERS TO THE HOLY SEE

Contents

Introduction 3

Fatima: Peace from War 7

Our Lady Appears: May to October 1917 15

Our Lady of Fatima and the Rosary 27

Message of Fatima, 1917 - 1939 35

Message of Fatima: 1939 - 1958 (Pius XII) 41

Message of Fatima: John XXIII and Paul VI 56

John Paul II consecrates Russia, 1984 65

John Paul II's teaching on Fatima 73

INTRODUCTION

Above the High Altar in the Basilica of our Lady of the Rosary at Fatima - very close to the precise spot where, on 13 October 1917, the Blessed Virgin revealed, "I am the Lady of the Rosary" - hangs a painting which depicts Our Lady bringing her Message to the three little shepherds, who had been prepared for her coming in the previous year by their encounter with Christ in the Eucharist, brought to them by the Angel of Portugal. In the centre of the picture stands Our Lady, looking down on the Bishop of Leiria-Fatima and the three children, who are shown receiving the Eucharist from the Angel of Portugal; and behind Our Lady's left shoulder can be glimpsed the dome of St Peter's Basilica, Rome, and three Popes closely associated with Fatima prior to John Paul II: Pius XII, the "Pope of Fatima"; John XXIII, the first Pope to have visited Fatima, in May 1956, when he was Cardinal Patriarch of Venice; and Paul VI, who made three separate references to Fatima at the Second Vatican Council, and became the first Pope to travel to Fatima as a pilgrim, in May 1967, the 50th anniversary year of the apparitions.

This scene effectively depicts one of the more remarkable aspects of the apparitions of Fatima: the association, from the very outset, between the papacy, the message of Fatima, and the peace for the world sought by the Popes. This relationship has gradually unfolded through the steadily increasing approval shown by the Popes to Our Lady's message, culminating, as will be seen, in the important acts and new teaching on the message by Pope John Paul II, which have brought a clearer understanding of its relevance to the Church's apostolic mission on the verge of the third millennium.

Cardinal Ratzinger summarised the continuing papal approval of Fatima in an interview at Fatima, on 13 October 1996: "In the most solemn way possible, three Popes (Pius XII, Paul VI and John Paul II) have already recognised Fatima and were totally committed to this devotion... more and more we see how this message speaks ever more urgently to the men and women of today" (*The Seers of Fatima*, Oct-Dec 1996, pp. 6, 7).

Pius XII

Pius XII, who reigned from 2 March 1939 to 9 October 1958, features in the painting because he was the first Pope publicly to manifest the Church's approval of Our Lady's message; and in a certain sense one can say that his association with the apparitions spans the whole drama of Fatima across this century, extending forwards, on the one hand, to the present pontificate of John Paul II, and on the other, reaching back to commence with his personal, if indirect, relationship with the very first apparition of Our Lady. For it is a remarkable fact that at the same moment Our Lady first appeared to the three little shepherds, on 13 May 1917, Mgr Eugenio Pacelli, the future

Pius XII and "Pope of Fatima", as he was destined to become known, was being consecrated Bishop in the Sistine Chapel.

Three years after his election, Pius XII became the first Pope formally to declare the Church's approval of the message of Fatima, by his act consecrating the world to the Immaculate Heart of Mary, which he carried out on 31 October 1942; this was followed by a second act of approval on 13 May 1946, when Pius XII's legate, Cardinal Masella, crowned the statue of Our Lady in the Capelinha (Portuguese for "little chapel") as Queen of Peace and Queen of the World, placing on her head a costly crown of gold and precious stones donated by the women of Portugal.

John Paul II

About forty years later, the crown that is so closely linked to Pope Pius XII was to receive a unique new 'jewel' as a memento of Pope John Paul II's extraordinary association with Our Lady of Fatima. On the 13th of each month from May to October, this crown is brought out and placed on the head of the celebrated statue in the Capelinha, which is then processed up to the outside altar for Mass, in a beautiful and moving ceremony commemorating the apparitions of Our Lady. Anyone who is present in Fatima on one of these dates, standing in a position to look through the arms of the crown, will be able to see, attached to the underside of the orb, and with its tip pointing downwards, one of the bullets that were fired at Pope John Paul II outside St Peter's Basilica, Rome, on 13 May 1981, feast day of Our Lady of Fatima and the precise anniversary of Our Lady's first apparition.

On several occasions, the Pope has publicly thanked Our Lady for having intervened to save his life at that moment of mortal danger when "I felt your helpful presence at my side", as he stated in his Act of Entrustment to the Mother of God at Fatima, on 13 May 1991. When, some time after the outrage, the Pope met his would-be-assassin in prison, Ali Agca was not afraid to ask him: "Why didn't you die? I know that my aim was true". "One hand fired the shot, another guided it", came John Paul II's memorable reply (cited in Fatima, Russia and Pope John Paul II, p. 9). And in a recent interview at Fatima, on 13 October 1996, Cardinal Ratzinger stated, "the fact that the Pope survived is really a miracle and the date on which it all happened is in itself significant" (*The Seers of Fatima*, Oct-Dec 1996, p. 7).

This event, surely unprecedented in the history of the papacy, led the Pope to a deeper involvement with Fatima. Meanwhile, primary sources reveal that the papacy has a closer and more significant association with the origins of Our Lady's apparitions than the providential consecration of the future Pius XII on 13 May 1917.

FATIMA: PEACE FROM WAR

Our Lady appeared at Fatima at a critical moment in history, when the European powers were deadlocked in frightful carnage at the height of the First World War. From the moment of his election on 3 September 1914, Pope Benedict XV refused to condemn either side, denounced the war as "a monstrous spectacle... the suicide of civilised Europe", and strenuously sought to negotiate peace, but in vain.

The Angel of Peace

But in the midst of man's inferno of war, God was mysteriously and wonderfully at work. It was in the spring of 1916 that the "Angel of Peace", as he called himself, appeared to three shepherd children at Fatima: Lucia, aged nine and the last child of a family of six, and her two cousins, Francisco, aged seven, and Jacinta, aged six. The Loca do Cabeco, where the Angel appeared, always makes a deep impression on pilgrims, since here the rather wild countryside has remained largely unchanged, and imparts a strong sense of the supernatural that was experienced by the children, as Lucia vividly relates in her Memoirs. By contrast, the Cova da Iria, where Our Lady appeared barely a mile away, has been transformed almost beyond recognition.

The Angel appeared "in the form of a young man", writes Lucia, "transparent, and brighter than crystal pierced by the rays of the sun", and, as will be seen, it is particularly significant that he called himself "*the Angel of Peace*". "Led by a supernatural impulse", says Lucia, "we repeated the words which we heard him say: My God, I believe, I adore, I hope and I love you! I ask pardon of You for those who do not believe, do not adore, do not hope and do not love You !"

The Angel repeated this prayer three times, and then said: "Pray thus. The Hearts of Jesus and Mary are attentive to the voice of your supplications."

This prayer, which is sublime in its intention and its childlike openness of heart and simplicity, constitutes the perfect prayer-response God desires from us, firstly to fulfill the purpose of our creation - to know, love and serve God - and secondly, to make reparation for the sin of those who reject Him. As such, especially in its second part, the prayer embodies the whole *raison d'etre* of Our Lady's apparitions; for it is the grave consequences of the open rejection of God by society, which brought down Our Lady from heaven with her merciful message of salvation for sinners and conditional promise of peace in the world. Finally, as with the 'Our Father', this prayer must be one that God specially desires to hear in our hearts and on our lips, since it comes not from man but from the Heart of God Himself, on the lips of His '*Angel of Peace*'.

About July 1916, the Angel appeared to the children for the second time and said: "Pray! Pray very much! The Hearts of Jesus and Mary have designs of mercy upon you... Make of everything you can a sacrifice, and offer it to God as an act of reparation for the sins by which he is offended, and in supplication for the conversion of sinners. You will thus draw down peace upon your country (emphasis added). I am its Angel Guardian, the Angel of Portugal. Above all, accept and bear with submission the suffering which the Lord will send you".

"These words were indelibly impressed upon our minds", continued Lucia, writing some twenty-five years later, in her Fourth and most complete Memoir. "They were like a light which made us understand who God is, how He loves us and desires to be loved, the value of sacrifice, how pleasing it is to Him and how, on account of it, He grants the grace of conversion to sinners".

Towards the end of September, the Angel appeared for the third and final time, holding a chalice which received drops of blood from the host above it. Leaving the host and chalice suspended in the air, the Angel knelt beside the children and taught them this moving prayer of Eucharistic reparation:

"Most Holy Trinity, Father, Son and Holy Spirit, I adore You profoundly, and I offer You the most precious Body, Blood, Soul and Divinity of Jesus Christ, present in all the tabernacles of the world, in reparation for the outrages, sacrileges and indifference with which He Himself is offended. And through the infinite merits of His most Sacred Heart, and the Immaculate Heart of Mary, I beg of You the conversion of poor sinners".

The Angel then gave the host to Lucia and the chalice to Jacinta and Francisco, saying as he did so: "Take and drink the Body and Blood of Jesus Christ, horribly outraged by ungrateful men. Repair their crimes and console your God" (*Fatima in Lucia's Own Words*, pp. 150-154).

Hence, in the short space of a few months in 1916, the Angel had initiated the little shepherds into deep mysteries of the Faith, in order to prepare them for the more extensive communications they were to receive from Our Lady in the following year.

Fatima's Message

Like the two prayers of the Angel, Our Lady's message is primarily a strong appeal to personal conversion and sanctification through practising in one's daily life the faith, worship and devotions of the Church; and it is noteworthy that in recent years, the Bishop of Leiria-Fatima has been emphasising the importance of living the message day by day. But, enlarging on the theme of the Angel's prayers, Our Lady's message is equally a strong call to labour apostolically for the salvation of all, and especially for those who deny and reject

God and the precepts of the Gospel, and thereby risk losing their souls for eternity. In both these respects, the message of Fatima constitutes God's merciful response to the sins of mankind by which He is increasingly offended, and the manifestation of His ardent desire for the conversion of sinners through the maternal solicitude of His holy Mother.

Set in the particular context of the First World War, the message of Fatima, with its conditional prophecy of a worse war to follow, reminds mankind of the constant teaching of Scripture, the Magisterium and the Second Vatican Council, that serious sin, above all, the sin of the conscious public rejection of God by society, leads to war.

It was precisely this sin of the rejection and denial of God, that was defined by Popes Benedict XV and Pius XII as the root cause of the First and Second World Wars; and this teaching of his predecessors was re-affirmed by Pope John Paul II, on the 50th Anniversary of the Outbreak of the Second World War.

Papal endorsements and teaching

Meanwhile, in his first official act endorsing the message of Fatima, Pope Pius XII consecrated the world to the Immaculate Heart of Mary in October 1942, imploring peace from God through the intercession of the Queen of Peace and Mother of Mercy. Next, Pope Paul VI made three separate references to Fatima at the Second Vatican Council, and travelled to Fatima as a humble pilgrim, in May 1967, to ask for the gift of God's peace from the Queen of Peace, because the world was in danger.

Finally, John Paul II has demonstrated, by two events of great importance in his pontificate, that the message of Fatima has a special relevance to the life of the Church today, as it prepares to enter the third millennium.

Firstly, on 25 March 1984, John Paul II consecrated the world to the Immaculate Heart of Mary in front of the statue of Our Lady of Fatima on the steps of St Peter's Basilica, Rome, praying: "from famine and war, deliver us; from nuclear war, from incalculable self-destruction, from every kind of war, deliver us". Then in 1990, following the changes in the former Soviet Union, the Bishop of Leiria-Fatima stated: "It is lawful to think that everything which surprisingly has happened in Eastern and Central Europe - religious liberty recognised by governments, institution of the sacred hierarchy, respect for the fundamental rights of the human person - can be attributed to the intervention of Our Lady, solicitous Mother of all men and all peoples". It would appear that these changes have improved the prospects for peace and reduced the risk of war.

And secondly, when he made his first pilgrimage to Fatima in May 1982, John Paul II delivered a homily which is of particular importance, because in it, for the first time in the history of Fatima, the Pope, guided by the Holy Spirit, has issued a substantial body of teaching on the message of Fatima.

FATIMA: PEACE FROM WAR

Hence, in the light of this homily, we may learn what is God's will for us in the message Our Lady delivered to the Church and the world at Fatima, at this important moment in salvation history, when the Church is preparing for the third millennium.

Briefly, John Paul II taught that "sin has made itself firmly at home in the world, and denial of God has become widespread in the ideologies, ideas and plans of human beings. But for this very reason the evangelical call to repentance and conversion, uttered in the Mother's message... is still more relevant than it was sixty-five years ago, still more urgent... If the Church has accepted the message of Fatima, it is above all because that message is... in its basic nucleus, a call to conversion and repentance, as in the Gospel".

Repentance signifies personal sorrow for and resolve to turn away from sin, conversion signifies turning towards and desire for a way of life pleasing to God. The fruit of this twofold action is true peace: that peace, first of all, which consists in union with God, the peace of Christ in the Eucharist; thereafter follows peace with one's family, one's neighbour, one's community. Then, in proportion as sin is driven out by the life of divine grace to which the message of Fatima calls us, true peace will arise and progressively extend throughout society, and the threat of war will be correspondingly diminished. As we will now see, it was immediately following Pope Benedict XV's urgent appeal to God for peace and an end to the First World War, that Our Lady came to Fatima with her maternal appeal for people to cease offending God by their sins, "because He is already so much offended... If what I say to you is done, many souls will be saved and there will be peace".

Benedict XV and World War I

In 1917, the war plunged into new depths of horror. Shells containing deadly gases were introduced, and owing to prolonged rain, the terrain in Belgium became a quagmire of mud, into which many of the wounded slowly sank, to die by drowning.

When he saw that all his attempts to negotiate peace between the belligerents came to naught, Benedict XV was finally moved to send out a memorable pastoral letter to the whole Catholic world, dated 5th May 1917, in which he urged all to pray fervently to the Sacred Heart of Jesus for peace, through the intercession of the Blessed Virgin Mary, "Mother of mercy and omnipotent by grace". At the same time he directed that the invocation "Queen of peace, pray for us" should be added to the Litany of Loreto.

Following this heartfelt appeal from the Pope, eight days later the Blessed Virgin appeared on 13th May to the three little shepherds in the Cova da Iria (the words signify "hollow of peace"), in the parish of Fatima, and already in her parting words to the children, the Holy Virgin brought an answer from heaven to the urgent appeal of Benedict XV.

OUR LADY APPEARS:
MAY TO OCTOBER 1917

The story of the sublime encounter of the three little shepherds with the holy Mother of God in the Cova da Iria, is told by Lucia, the surviving seer, in "Fatima in Lucia's Own Words." Anyone who wishes to savour in full the vivid details, recalled by Lucia's excellent memory, of the meetings between the gracious Queen of Heaven and the three little shepherds, should read this spiritual classic. Only brief extracts are included here, partly because the story has become so well known, but primarily because our object is to focus on one of the principal themes of the message of Fatima, which already begins to emerge in the first apparition of Our Lady on 13 May 1917.

13 May 1917

The Lady told them that she came from heaven, and that she wanted them to return to the same place, at the same time, on the 13th of each month for six months in succession. "Later on, I will tell you who I am and what I want ". The Lady said they would all go to heaven, and then asked the children:

"Are you willing to offer yourselves to God and bear all the sufferings He wills to send you, as an act of reparation for the conversion of sinners? - Yes, we are willing. - Then you are going to have much to suffer, but the grace of God will be your comfort ".

"As she pronounced these last words ...", writes Lucia, "Our Lady opened her hands for the first time, communicating to us a light so intense that, as it streamed from her hands, its rays penetrated our hearts and the innermost depths of our souls, making us see ourselves in God, Who was that light, more clearly than we see ourselves in the best of mirrors. Then, moved by an interior impulse that was also communicated to us, we fell on our knees, repeating in our hearts: O most Holy Trinity, I adore You! My God, my God, I love You in the Most Blessed Sacrament ".

Reflecting briefly on this scene, it is interesting to compare what the children were led to experience mystically through Mary, with the Holy Father's observations about Marian devotion in his book, *Crossing the Threshold of Hope*. "Thanks to St Louis de Montfort", he wrote, "I came to understand that true devotion to the Mother of God is actually Christocentric, indeed it is very profoundly rooted in the Mystery of the Blessed Trinity, and the mysteries of the Incarnation and Redemption... In regard to Marian devotion, each of us must understand that such devotion not only addresses a need of the heart, a sentimental inclination, but that it also corresponds to the objective truth about the Mother of God" (p. 213).

Then, just as this first apparition came to an end and Our Lady began to rise serenely towards the east into the immensity of space, Lucia records that she spoke to them again. In words which convey the impression that she was making a direct personal response to the urgent petition of Benedict XV, Our Lady said: "Pray the Rosary every day, in order to obtain peace for the world and the end of the war".

Our Lady requested daily recitation of the Rosary in each of her six apparitions. Moreover, in three of the six, she specifically linked the Rosary with peace and the end of the war: in July she repeated the request that she had used in May, in exactly the same words as above; and in September she said, "continue to pray the Rosary in order to obtain the end of the war".

Pope John Paul II recently confirmed the efficacy of the Rosary for these two intentions in his midday Angelus on 26 October 1997, when he stated:

"How many times in the course of history has the Church had recourse to this prayer, especially in particularly difficult moments. The Holy Rosary was a privileged means for averting the danger of war and obtaining the gift of peace from God. Did not the Blessed Virgin, when appearing to the three shepherd children in Fatima 80 years ago, ask that the Rosary be recited for the conversion of sinners and peace in the world?.. May Mary's Rosary help us to implore God for reconciliation and peace for all humanity". The Pope then invited all Christian families to pray the Rosary, because "world peace also comes through the peace of families, the basic cells of the great human family".

Further apparitions: June and July

In the June apparition, Our Lady said that she was going to take Jacinta and Francisco to heaven soon, but Lucia had a different mission. She was to learn to read because "you are to stay here some time longer. Jesus wishes to make use of you to make me known and loved. He wants to establish in the world devotion to my Immaculate Heart... Are you suffering a great deal? Don't lose heart. I will never forsake you. My Immaculate Heart will be your refuge and the way to lead you to God".

The children then saw themselves "as it were, immersed in God", in the light which came from Our Lady's hands. "In front of the palm of Our Lady's right hand was a heart encircled by thorns which pierced it. We understood that this was the Immaculate Heart of Mary, outraged by the sins of humanity, and seeking reparation".

In July, the children received the most complete of Our Lady's six separate communications. At the beginning of the apparition, she renewed her request for daily recitation of the Rosary, in exactly the same words that she had used in May, and just before leaving, she taught the children the well known prayer to be added at the end of each mystery: 'O my Jesus, forgive us, save us from the fire of hell. Lead all souls to heaven, especially those who are most in need'. She said that in October she would tell them who she was, and perform a miracle "for all to see and believe" (In October, indeed, the sun was seen to change colours and 'dance in the sky' by some 70,000 people). She taught them to make sacrifices for sinners, and when doing so, to pray: 'O my Jesus, it is for love of you, for the conversion of sinners, and in reparation for the sins committed against the Immaculate Heart of Mary'.

Next, Our Lady showed the children the vision of hell, described in the most vivid detail by Lucia in her memoirs. Finally, she foretold the unfolding of events in the course of this century. Note that peace is central to the theme of this remarkable prophecy, the words of which are printed in full in the following two paragraphs:

"You have seen hell where the souls of poor sinners go. To save them, God wishes to establish in the world devotion to my Immaculate Heart. If what I say to you is done, many souls will be saved, and there will be peace. The war (i.e., the First World War) is going to end; but if people do not cease offending God, a worse war [i.e., the Second World War) will break out during the pontificate of Pius XI. When you see a night illumined by an unknown light [this was the Aurora Borealis that was seen all over Europe on the night of 25-26 January 1938), know that this is the great sign given you by God that he is about to punish the world for its crimes, by means of war, famine, and persecutions of the Church and of the Holy Father.

To prevent this, I shall come to ask for the consecration of Russia to my Immaculate Heart (Pope John Paul II fulfilled this request on the steps of St Peter's Basilica, Rome, on 25 March 1984), and the Communion of Reparation on the First Saturdays [the Five First Saturdays devotion]. If my requests are heeded, Russia will be converted, and there will be peace; if not, she will spread her errors throughout the world, causing wars and persecutions of the Church. The good will be martyred, the Holy Father will have much to suffer, various nations will be annihilated. In the end, my Immaculate Heart will triumph. The Holy Father will consecrate Russia to me, and she will be converted, *and a period of peace will be granted to the world*. In Portugal, the dogma of the faith will always be preserved; etc... Do not tell this to anybody. Francisco, yes, you may tell him".

Final three apparitions

To summarise the final three apparitions, as regards the essence of the message of Fatima, Our Lady made one new request, in October, when she told them that "a chapel is to be built here in my honour". In August, she told the children once more: "Pray very much, and make sacrifices for sinners; for many souls go to hell, because there are none to sacrifice themselves and to pray for them"; and her very last words to the children in October also concerned sin: "do not offend the Lord our God any more, because He is already so much offended". Finally, in each of these three apparitions, Our Lady repeated just one request, for the daily recitation of the

Rosary, and in October she revealed: "I am the Lady of the Rosary" (*Fatima in Lucia's Own Words*, pp. 156-168).

As we have seen, the July apparition included each category of the different requests of Our Lady. All these requests are intended to remedy the problem of sin and effect the salvation of souls - the *raison d'etre* of the whole message - but her words further make it clear that it is people's freedom to heed her requests and "cease offending God", or not, upon which depends the issue of whether war or peace will prevail in the world.

It is interesting to note that "Fatima and Peace" was the theme chosen for the International Congress on 8-12 May 1992, organised by the Sanctuary of Fatima and the Catholic University of Portugal, to celebrate the opening of the Diamond Jubilee Anniversary Year of Our Lady's apparitions. "This event invites us to reflect on peace, which constitutes the kernel of the message of Fatima", stated the publicity brochure, and five major papers were delivered on subjects such as 'Fatima, the World and Peace', 'Fatima, Peace and Russia', and 'Peace in the Documents of Fatima and in Papal Messages'.

Accordingly, in the light of the above and other evidence it has been possible to consult, it seems one may conclude that the Blessed Virgin appeared at Fatima as a direct response to the urgent petition of Pope Benedict XV to the Sacred Heart of Jesus, for peace and an end to the First World War, through the intercession of the Mother of Mercies and Queen of Peace.

However, while views may differ about the papacy's association with the origins of Our Lady's apparitions at Fatima, once Our Lady's message had been revealed and made known, it is clear that it was the ensuing response of the papacy which formed the most important part of her comprehensive spiritual programme to obtain peace for the world.

Papal response to Fatima

The requests which the Blessed Virgin came to Fatima to convey to the Church through Lucia, can be divided into three different categories of response, the highest of which comprised a solemn act of consecration by the Pope as Chief Shepherd in union with all the Bishops, thereby signifying the union of the whole people of God, the Mystical Body of Christ. This act, which the Bishop of Leiria-Fatima has confirmed was fulfilled by John Paul II on 25 March 1984, on the steps of St Peter's Basilica, Rome, was carried out in response to the request from God conveyed by Our Lady when she came again to Lucia, on 13 June 1929, as she had promised in July 1917.

On the night of 13 June 1929, as Lucia relates in Appendix II of her memoirs, she was making a holy hour in the chapel. "Suddenly the whole chapel was illumined by a supernatural light, and above the altar appeared a cross of light, reaching to the ceiling. In a brighter light on the upper part of the cross could be seen the face of a man and his body as far as the waist; upon his breast was a dove of light; nailed to the cross was the body of another man. A little below the waist I could see a chalice and a large host suspended in the air, on to which drops of blood were falling from the face of Jesus Crucified and from the wound in His side. These drops ran down onto the host and fell into the chalice. Beneath the right arm of the cross was Our Lady and in her hand was her Immaculate Heart... with a crown of thorns and flames. Under the left arm of the cross, large letters, as if of crystal clear water which ran down upon the altar, formed these words: Grace and Mercy. I understood that it was the Mystery of the Most Holy Trinity which was shown to me, and I received lights about this mystery which I am not permitted to reveal. Our Lady then said to me:

'The moment has come in which God asks the Holy Father, in union with all the Bishops of the world to make the consecration of Russia to my Immaculate Heart, promising to save it by this means'" (*Fatima in Lucia's Own Words*, p. 200).

Five First Saturdays

The response next in importance, because it was linked with the Pope's act of consecration and centred on reception of the Sacraments of Penance and the Eucharist, was Our Lady's request for the Five First Saturdays Communion of Reparation.

Lucia recounts how this devotion was revealed to her at Pontevedra, in Appendix I of her memoirs (*Fatima in Lucia's own Words*, pp. 189-197). On 10 December 1925, Our Lady appeared to her with the Holy Child, and holding her heart encircled with thorns in her hand. The Holy Child said to her:

"Have compassion on the Heart of your most holy Mother, covered with thorns, with which ungrateful men pierce it at every moment, and there is no one to make an act of reparation to remove them". Then the most holy Virgin said:

"Look, my daughter, at my Heart, surrounded with thorns, with which ungrateful men pierce me at every moment by their blasphemies and ingratitude. You at least try to console me and say that I promise to assist at the hour of death, with the graces necessary for salvation, all those who, on the First Saturday of five consecutive months, shall confess, receive Holy Communion, recite five decades of the Rosary, and keep me company for fifteen minutes while meditating on the fifteen mysteries of the Rosary, with the intention of making reparation to me".

Later, on 29 May 1930, Our Lord explained to Lucia,
"...There are five ways in which people offend and blaspheme against the Immaculate Heart of Mary: "Blasphemies against the Immaculate Conception, against her Virginity, and against the divine Maternity and the refusal to recognise her as the Mother of all mankind; blasphemies by those who seek publicly to implant in the hearts of children indifference, contempt and even hatred against this Immaculate Mother, and by those who insult her directly in her sacred images". (*Memorias e Cartas da Irma Lucia* - Memoirs and Letters of Sister Lucia, in one volume, in Portuguese, French and English, edited by Antonio Martins, SJ; 1972, p. 409).

Our Lady linked her request for the Five First Saturdays devotion with her request for the Holy Father's act of consecration to her Immaculate Heart, which immediately preceded it; then, in her words which followed, Our Lady explained: "If my requests are heeded, Russia will be converted and there will be peace; if not, she will spread her errors throughout the world, causing wars and persecutions of the Church. The good will be martyred, the Holy Father will have much to suffer, various nations will be annihilated ..."

It is interesting to note how the principal features of this comparatively new devotion to the Immaculate Heart of Mary, are found in the devotion to the Sacred Heart of Jesus which was revealed to St Margaret Mary, 1673-75. Through St Margaret Mary, Our Lord promised the grace of final repentance to all who received Communion on nine First Fridays consecutively: "they shall not die under my displeasure nor without receiving the Sacraments". Our Lord also complained of men's ingratitude, for which He asked St Margaret Mary to console Him "as far as you are able", and requested a feast in honour of His Heart and "the reception of Communion on that day in reparation for the outrages It has received while exposed on the Altars".

In the Five First Saturdays devotion, the importance of the Rosary is such that, after Confession and a Communion of Reparation, Our Lady also asks for the recitation of five decades of the Rosary, and fifteen minutes meditation on the fifteen mysteries of the Rosary, with the intention of making reparation to her.

Prayer and Sacrifice

In the final category of her requests, Our Lady asks people to participate in the work of salvation by praying very much, especially the daily recitation of the Rosary, and by offering up the ordinary circumstances of their daily lives, in the form of sacrifices and whatever sufferings God wills to send them, for love of Jesus, for the conversion of sinners, and in reparation for sins against the Immaculate Heart of Mary.

Our Lady of Fatima and the Rosary

As we have seen, at Fatima Our Lady placed particular emphasis on the Rosary, by asking for its daily recitation in the one and only request that she repeated in all six of her apparitions. Furthermore, in three out of the six apparitions she stated that daily recitation of the Rosary was the means of obtaining peace for the world and the end of the war; and finally in October she revealed: "I am the Lady of the Rosary". What does the Church teach us about this prayer of the Rosary that is so dear to Our Lady?

Popes urge Prayer of Rosary

In 1569, Pope St Pius V explained and in a certain sense established the traditional form of the Rosary. In 1571, the same Pope instituted the Feast of the Rosary on the first Sunday in October, in thanksgiving for the victory on that day of Don John of Austria over the Turkish fleet, at the battle of Lepanto. After a further victory over the Turks, on 5 August 1716, at the battle of Peterwardein in Hungary, Pope Clement XI raised the feast of the Rosary on 7 October to universal celebration.

More than fifty Popes have urged the faithful to have recourse to Our Lady's Rosary, and from Leo XIII to John Paul II it is the form of extra-liturgical prayer they have most frequently recommended. Pope Leo XIII issued a record number of twelve encyclicals on the Rosary in the period from 1883 to 1901, twice asking that it be recited daily, as Our Lady was to do when she appeared only a few years later at Fatima. Leo XIII also added the invocation "Queen of the Most Holy Rosary" to the Litany of Loreto.

Leo XIII's successor was Pope St Pius X. In his testament, a large part of which was devoted to the Rosary, the Pope encouraged the faithful to pray the Rosary because, in his words: "The Rosary is the most beautiful and the most rich in graces of all prayers, it is the prayer that touches most the Heart of the Mother of God... and if you wish peace to reign in your homes, recite the family Rosary".

Shortly after his election in October 1978, Pope John Paul II said "the Rosary is my favourite prayer... marvellous in its simplicity and its profundity". More recently, in his message to the Bishop of Leiria-Fatima, on 1 October 1997, the Pope urged the faithful to "recite the Rosary every day. I earnestly urge Pastors to pray the Rosary and to teach people in their Christian communities how to pray it... for the faithful and courageous fulfilment of the human and Christian duties proper to each one's state".

The Pope summarised the meaning of praying the Rosary in the following words, at his General Audience of 29 October 1978: "Against the background of the words, Ave Maria, the principal episodes of Christ's life pass before the eyes of the soul. They consist of the sum of the joyful, sorrowful and glorious mysteries, and put us in living fellowship with Jesus through, we can say, his Mother's heart. At the same time, in these decades of the Rosary, our hearts can contain all the events making up the life of the individual, the family, the nation, the Church, the human race; things that happen to us, to our neighbour and particularly to those who are nearest to us, those whom we hold dearest. So the simple prayer of the Rosary keeps time with the rhythm of human life".

Valuable instruction on the correct method of praying the Rosary was given by Pope Paul VI, in his Apostolic Exhortation *Marialis Cultus*, on the Right Ordering and Development of Devotion to the Blessed Virgin Mary, issued on 2 February 1974. The Pope said that in addition to praise and petition, it was important to retain the element of contemplation, for "without this, the Rosary is a body without a soul, and its recitation is in danger of becoming a repetition of mechanical formulas... By its nature the recitation of the Rosary calls for a quiet rhythm and a lingering pace, helping the individual to meditate on the mysteries of the Lord's life as seen through the eyes of her who was closest to the Lord" (No. 47).

On several occasions, John Paul II has explained why the Rosary is important in terms of living one's faith day by day. In the first place, he described the Rosary as a "compendium (or summary) of the whole Gospel", using the phrase of his predecessor, Pius XII, in his midday Angelus on 26 October 1997; on the same occasion he also reminded the faithful of Paul VI's teaching in *Marialis Cultus*, that "as a Gospel prayer centred on the mystery of the Redemptive Incarnation, the Rosary is therefore a prayer with a clearly Christological orientation" (No. 46).

The secret of preserving one's inheritance of faith, John Paul II taught in his address at Fatima on 12 May 1982, was "no longer a secret: pray, pray very much, recite the Rosary every day"; and in his homily, on 13th May, he taught that in the Rosary, "which can rightly be defined as Mary's prayer,... she herself prays with us. The Rosary prayer embraces the problems of the Church, of the See of Peter, the problems of the whole world".

Vatican II

Moving on to the Second Vatican Council, it is clear that the following passage in the Dogmatic Constitution on the Church, *Lumen Gentium*, endorses this devotion. "The sacred Council.. reminds all the Church's children to give generous encouragement to the cult of the Blessed Virgin... to value highly the practices and exercises of piety in her regard which have had in the course of the ages, the recommendation of the Magisterium... the faithful must bear in mind that real devotion does not consist in sterile, transitory emotion nor in idle credulity, but that it has its starting point in the true faith which bring us to recognise the excellence of God's Mother, and rouses us to a son's love for our mother and to imitation of her virtues" (No. 67).

The Saints

The Rosary has been spread by great saints such as St Peter Canisius, St Alphonsus Liguori, and St Louis de Montfort. In his book entitled *The Secret of the Rosary*, de Montfort wrote: "Never will anyone who says his Rosary every day become a formal heretic or be led astray by the devil". The reason for this, he explained, is that the Rosary gradually gives us a perfect knowledge and love of Jesus, purifies our souls from sin, and makes it easy for us to practise virtue. St Francis de Sales overcame a temptation to despair through praying the Rosary every day, and St Bonaventure said that Mary will greet you with grace if you greet her with the Hail Mary.

Sr Lucia

We also have an important testimony on the Rosary from Sr Lucia - the seer chosen by Heaven to convey to the Church Our Lady's requests for daily recitation of the Rosary, who was shown divine mysteries in the light that came from Our Lady's hands, in May and June, and who was told by Our Lady in June, "Jesus wishes to make use of you to make me known and loved. I will never forsake you. My Immaculate Heart will be your refuge and the way to lead you to God".

In a letter to a religious, Sr Lucia wrote that all the prayers of the Rosary came from Heaven, and were dictated by the Father, the Son and the Holy Spirit.

The Hail Mary is "completely impregnated both with a Trinitarian and a Eucharistic sense... It is a Trinitarian prayer because Mary was the first living temple of the most Holy Trinity, evident from the words of the Angel: The Holy Spirit shall come upon thee, the power of the Most High shall overshadow thee, and therefore the Holy One to be born of thee shall be called the Son of God". (Lk. 1:35). It is also Eucharistic. Mary is the first living tabernacle wherein the Father enclosed His Son, the Word made flesh. Her Immaculate Heart is the first monstrance to hold Him. Her breast and her arms were the first altar on which the Father exposed His Son for adoration ..

After the Sacred Liturgy of the Eucharist, the prayer of the Rosary is what best fosters within our spirit the growth of the virtues of faith, hope and charity. It is the spiritual bread of souls... We cannot hopefully expect a great number of souls to assist at daily Mass, but we can hope to bring a greater number of them to recite the daily Rosary. This practice will preserve and increase their faith, due to the prayer life it fosters, and to the mysteries of our Redemption which are remembered in each decade. That is why the devil has mounted against it such a great attack" (*Letter of Sr Lucia to Mother Martins*, 16 September 1970).

Power of the Rosary

Father Patrick Peyton, CSC, was famous for spreading devotion to the Holy Rosary throughout the world. His motto was: "the family that prays together stays together", and in his Rosary Prayer Book, he explains that "in St John's Gospel (1: 11-12) we have a summary of the heart, soul and meaning of the fifteen mysteries of the Rosary: "He came unto His own" (the Joyful Mysteries); "And His own received Him not" (the Sorrowful Mysteries); "But to all who did accept Him He gave power to become children of God" (the Glorious Mysteries).

Finally, the famous American preacher, Bishop Fulton Sheen, said "the power of the Rosary is beyond description", and to illustrate this truth he told the following story of a Jew he knew in World War I, who was in a shell hole on the Western Front with four Austrian soldiers. "Suddenly, one shell killed his four companions. He took a Rosary from the hands of one of them and began to say it. He knew it by heart for he had heard others say it so often. At the end of the first decade, he felt an inner warning to leave that shell hole. He crawled through much mud and muck and threw himself into another. At that moment, a shell hit the first hole, where he had been lying. Four more times, exactly the same experience...

He promised then to give his life to Our Lord and to His Blessed Mother if he should be saved. After the war more sufferings came to him; his family was burned by Hitler, but his promise lingered on. Recently, I baptised him - and the grateful soldier is now preparing to study for the priesthood" (Fulton Sheen, *The World's First Love*, pp. 219-220).

MESSAGE OF FATIMA: 1917 - 1939

Let us now briefly trace the development of the message of Fatima, from 1917 to the election of Pope Pius XII on 2nd March 1939.

Benedict XV

Is it possible that Pope Benedict XV knew of Our Lady's apparitions at Fatima? In his book, *More About Fatima*, the Portuguese historian, Fr J. da Cruz, C. S. Sp, mentions two important communications from Benedict XV to the Portuguese hierarchy, which appear to indicate that the Pope had been informed of the events which had taken place at Fatima in 1917.

At that date, the parish of Fatima belonged to the diocese of Lisbon, and the Church in Portugal was suffering a period of extreme persecution from the anti-clerical regime, which had toppled the ancient Catholic monarchy in 1908 and installed a Republic in October 1910. Principally for this reason, the clergy of the diocese were strictly forbidden by the patriarchal curia in Lisbon to take any part in the remarkable events at Fatima, news of which had spread like wildfire over the whole country. However, after the miracle of the sun on 13 October 1917, the parish priest was compelled to take action by the testimony of thousands of people who had witnessed the super-natural phenomena, and the extent to which pilgrimages to the Cova da Iria and a cult of Our Lady had begun to spring up spontaneously. Fr Ferreira wrote urgently for guidance to Lisbon, and in its reply of 3 November, the curia authorised him to conduct a painstaking enquiry into the facts.

According to Fr da Cruz, it was "doubtless as a result of these weighty events" that Pope Benedict XV re-established the ancient diocese of Leiria, by a brief of 17 January 1918, and incorporated into it the parish of Fatima. Three months later, in reply to a report he had received from the Portuguese Bishops, Benedict XV wrote on 29 April that he had always hoped the situation of the Church in Portugal was only passing, because the people's ardent devotion to the Immaculate Conception merited an extraordinary aid for their country from the Mother of God (Fr J. da Cruz, *More About Fatima*, pp 102, 106). It seems probable, then, that Benedict XV may have been aware of the miraculous events at Fatima, almost from the outset.

Pius XI acts on Fatima

Benedict XV was succeeded by Pope Pius XI on 6 February 1922, and five years later, by a rescript dated 21 January 1927, as Fr J. Cacella tells us, the Sacred Congregation of Rites granted the faculty for celebrating the Votive Mass of the Most Holy Rosary to the Sanctuary of Fatima (Fr J. Cacella, *The*

Wonders of Fatima, New York, 1948, p. 46). Fr de Marchi adds that this privilege was accorded following the first visit to Fatima of the Apostolic Nuncio together with the Bishop of Leiria-Fatima, three months previously, in October 1926 (Fr J. de Marchi, IMC, *Fatima from the Beginning*, 1988, p. 227).

This authorisation for the Votive Mass of the Holy Rosary was the first official act by the Holy See in favour of the supernatural events at Fatima, and it was accorded nearly four years before the Bishop of Leiria-Fatima issued his Pastoral Letter on 13 October 1930, in which he declared that the visions of the children in the Cova da Iria were worthy of credence, and permitted the cult of Our Lady of Fatima. Meanwhile, in June 1927, ten years after the apparitions, the bishop carried out his first official public act at Fatima, when he solemnly blessed the Stations of the Cross along the road into Fatima from Batalha, and from then on Mass was celebrated daily in the Cova da Iria and the Blessed Sacrament reserved.

Then on 6 December 1929, almost a year before the Bishop of Leiria-Fatima issued his formal approval of the apparitions, Pius XI personally blessed at the Vatican the statue of Our Lady of Fatima which had been donated to the Portuguese Seminary in Rome. Thereafter, as Pius XII recorded in his consecration of the world on 31 October 1942, in the Apostolic Letter '*Ex officiosis Litteris*' which he issued in 1934, Pius XI "attested to the extraordinary benefits which the Mother of God had recently accorded to Portugal".

In thanksgiving for the formal approval of the cult of Our Lady of Fatima, a national pilgrimage was held on 13 May 1931. An estimated half a million pilgrims were present as the whole Portuguese episcopate, led by the Cardinal Patriarch of Lisbon, consecrated their country to the Immaculate Heart of Mary - the first of three acts of national consecration, that were repeated in 1938 and 1940, and secured the preservation of Portugal in peace, as will be seen subsequently. The ceremonies were attended by the Apostolic Nuncio from Lisbon, who returned to preside over the pilgrimage of 13 May in the following year.

Sr Lucia's writings

A few years later, an event took place which led to Lucia writing her first account of the apparitions. On 12 September 1935, the mortal remains of Jacinta were taken from Vila Nova da Ourem to the cemetery of Fatima, and when the coffin was opened, it was found that her face had remained intact. Various photographs were taken, and the Bishop sent one to Lucia, who at that time was a Dorothean nun in the convent of Pontevedra. On 17 November, she wrote to thank the Bishop, and in expressing her great joy at seeing again the closest friend of her childhood, she vividly recounted some stories of their times together. Touched, the Bishop asked her to write down everything she could remember about her cousin, and so it came about that on Christmas Day 1935, Lucia finished the first of what was to become four separate memoirs, each one disclosing something more of the apparitions. The seer wrote with a certain reluctance and out of obedience to the Bishop of Leiria-Fatima, since this for her was the expression of God's will. The fourth and last memoir, the longest and most complete account, was finished on 8 December 1941.

Lucia's account is "the richest, most comprehensive and vivid witness to the happenings in the Cova da Iria that we possess", as the editor, Fr L. Kondor, SVD, says in his preface. She describes the marvellous supernatural events with spontaneous charm and vitality, and an astonishing recall of detail, as if they had happened only yesterday. But the story of how Lucia was led to write this work, which is both a spiritual treasure as well as a vitally important historical record, aptly illustrates an unusual characteristic of the Fatima revelations which appears to be part of God's providential plan: that Our Lady's message gradually becomes known in the course of time, and thereafter is progressively assimilated into the life of the Church through the normal processes of discernment and response. One can see the same process at work with regard to the subsequent publication of Lucia's memoirs. Whereas the first complete account of the apparitions in Portuguese was written down by 1941, almost 25 years after the apparitions, *Fatima in Lucia's Own Words*, the current authorised English version of all four Memoirs, was not published until 1976 - almost 60 years after the apparitions, when the seer was 69! The work has become a spiritual classic in the life of the seer, but this edition was not to remain her last word on the subject.

For at the request of the Rector of the Sanctuary, Lucia, who was 90 years old in March 1997, has recently added a Fifth Memoir, on the life of her father, which was first published in English in 1995; and since then she has added a Sixth Memoir, on the life of her mother, which awaits translation and publication in English.

Likewise, the Sanctuary of Fatima is preparing the full official account of the marvellous supernatural occurrences described in such vivid detail by Lucia, and the subsequent impact of the message of Fatima throughout the Church and the world in the troubled twentieth century. However, apparently the work will be so extensive that it is unlikely to be published until some years into the third millennium.

Message of Fatima: 1939 - 1958
(Pius XII)

Following the death of Pius XI on 10 February 1939, Pius XII was crowned Pope on 12th March. He became known as "the Pope of Fatima", partly because he was consecrated Bishop on 13 May 1917, at the precise moment Our Lady first began to appear to the three little shepherds at Fatima, and partly because he was the first Pope publicly to accept and respond to the message of Fatima.

Six months later Britain and France declared war on Germany, a few days after Germany invaded Poland on 1 September. But had not Our Lady foretold, in July 1917, that if people did not cease offending God, a worse war would break out "during the pontificate of Pius XI?" In response to this difficulty, Lucia has always insisted that Our Lady mentioned Pius XI by name, and that in fact the Second World War began in March 1938, with Hitler's invasion and annexation of Austria - the Anschluss.

Sign of World War II

On the night of Tuesday 25th January 1938, about seven weeks before Hitler invaded Austria on 12 March, people all over a vast area of Europe watched in awe and amazement as an unprecedented display of the Aurora Borealis filled the sky. The Daily Telegraph of Wednesday 26th January 1938 carried a report of several columns on the brilliant spectacle that had been seen on the previous night. Normally only visible in northern latitudes, "last night's display was of such an intensity as to be seen throughout Britain, Holland, Belgium, Portugal, Italy, Switzerland and as far south as Vienna... The display began about 6.30. Its length varied between four hours in some parts of Britain to 30 minutes in others. The sky was illumined by a crimson glow which deepened to violet. Then two glowing red arcs formed from which brilliant white flashes like searchlight beams shot continually". The New York Times of the same date reported that the Aurora was seen as far afield as Gibraltar and Bermuda.

Whatever the scientific explanation of the phenomenon, Lucia had no doubt that this was the "unknown light... the great sign given you by God that He is about to punish the world for its crimes by means of war, famine, and persecutions of the Church and the Holy Father". Our Lady had warned that these evils would arise, if people do not cease offending God".

War as a consequence of sin

Let us reflect for a moment on these words of Our Lady. In essence, she is saying that it is people's unwillingness and refusal to give up their sins, which ultimately leads God to permit such evils as a punishment for resistance to and refusal of His grace and mercy. When Our Lady issued this grave warning, out of her deep maternal concern for the salvation of souls being lost through sin, she was neither formulating some new doctrine, nor seeking to bring souls to repentance purely through fear of future evils. The Mother of God was reminding us of the warning in Scripture: "What causes wars and fighting among you? Is it not your passions that are at war in your members? You desire and do not have, so you kill". (James 4:1, 2; cf. Is 1:16-20)

The same teaching is found in the Pastoral Constitution on the Church, *Gaudium et Spes* (No. 78.6): "Insofar as men are sinners the dangers of war hangs over them till the coming of Christ"; and in No. 83 the text says that war thrives on those factors which cause dissensions among men, the deeper reasons for which are "human envy, mistrust, pride and other selfish passions".

It should also be noted that Popes Benedict XV and Pius XII both taught that sin was the cause of the First and Second World Wars.

In his Encyclical *Ad Beatissimi Apostolorum*, dated 1 November 1914, Benedict XV wrote that "there is another evil raging in the very inmost heart of human society... which may rightly be considered to be the root cause of the present awful war. Ever since the precepts and practices of Christian wisdom ceased to be observed in the ruling of States, it followed that, as they contained the peace and stability of institutions, the very foundations of States necessarily began to be shaken" (*The Pope and the People*, CTS, 1932, p. 204).

Similarly, in his *Address to the World*, on Christmas Day 1941, Pope Pius XII identified the cause of the Second World War as "the unhappy spectacle of a gradual apostasy from Christianity... a religious anaemia has spread like a plague, creating in souls a moral void... who can wonder that so radical an opposition to the principles of Christian doctrine has finally resulted in a violent clash of internal and external tensions, and so caused the appalling destruction of life and property of which we are now the unhappy witnesses?.." (*The Pope speaks to the World*, CTS, 1942, pp. 4-6).

Fifty years on

Half a century later, Pope John Paul II issued an Apostolic Letter on the 50th Anniversary of the Outbreak of the Second World War, dated 27 August 1989, which was addressed not only to the Church, but also to those in Government and to all people of good will. In this Letter the Pope stated: "It is our duty before God to remember these tragic events... to learn from the past, so that never again will there arise a set of factors capable of triggering a similar conflagration". John Paul II records that, from the date of his election on 2 March 1939, Pope Pius XII "did not fail to issue an appeal for that peace which everyone agreed was seriously threatened. A few days before the outbreak of hostilities, on 24 August 1939, he spoke prophetic words that still resound today: 'Once again a grave hour is at hand for the whole human family... The peril is imminent, but there is still time. Nothing is lost with peace. Everything can be lost with war'".

Commenting on the issues raised by the Second World War, John Paul II wrote: "In returning to the history of those six terrible years, it is only right that one regard with horror the contempt with which man was held... the moral abyss into which contempt for God and thus for man plunged the world fifty years ago... the collapse of Christian values that led to yesterday's moral failures, must make us vigilant as to the way the Gospel is proclaimed and lived out today. Unfortunately, we must observe that in many areas of existence modern man thinks, lives and acts as if God did not even exist. In this we find lurking the same danger that was present yesterday: that man will be handed over to the power of man. It is to Mary, the Queen of Peace, that I entrust all mankind, confiding to her maternal intercession this history in which we all have a part to play" (printed in *The Second World War*, CTS, 1989, pp. 8, 12, 18, 19).

In another message on the same occasion, the Pope said "the historical reality of the Second World War is even more terrible than any terms that might ever be used to describe it", (*The Second World War*, p. 26). Had not Our Lady indeed warned that "if people do not cease offending God, a worse one will break out..."? Finally, in a potent phrase in his book, *Crossing the Threshold of Hope* (p. 150), John Paul II summed up the two World Wars, and the concentration and extermination camps, as "events that clash profoundly with the truth of the Gospel".

Portugal's protection

Meanwhile, on 8 December 1940 the Bishops of Portugal carried out the third consecration of their country to the Immaculate Heart of Mary in the cathedral of Lisbon, in response to a request they had received from Sr Lucia. In a letter dated 2 December 1940 which, in obedience to her spiritual director, she wrote to Pope Pius XII, Sr Lucia explained the reason for carrying out this act as follows: "Most Holy Father, if in the union of my soul with God I have not been deceived, Our Lord promises a special protection to our country in this war, due to the consecration of the nation to the Immaculate Heart of Mary by the Bishops of Portugal, and as proof of the graces that would be granted to other nations if, like Portugal, they had been consecrated to it".

At the 8th Fatima Congress, at Kevelaer, Germany in September 1977, the Cardinal Patriarch of Lisbon gave the following testimony to that act of consecration: "I can say that it was the consecration made in Fatima to the Immaculate Heart of Mary by the Portuguese Bishops in 1931 and 1938 that defended Portugal from the common peril, then so close to its borders (the Cardinal was referring to two events in Spain, first the Communist uprising and then the Civil War, which had inflicted grave damage and loss of life on the Church). It was the same consecration, renewed in 1940, which saved Portugal from the horrors of the Second World War..."

Pius XII's Act of Consecration

Two years later, in the silver jubilee year of Our Lady's apparitions and of his own consecration as bishop, Pope Pius XII carried out the first official, public act signifying the papacy's approval and acceptance of the message of Fatima, when he consecrated the world to the Immaculate Heart of Mary, on 31 October 1942. In the course of this act, the Pope recalled her "whom one of our predecessors in the First World War ordered to be invoked as Queen of Peace", and prayed:

"O Mother of Mercy, obtain for us peace from God, and first of all, those graces which can convert the hearts of men in a moment, the graces which prepare, facilitate and assure peace. Queen of Peace, pray for us, and give to the world at war the peace for which people long..."

In a letter to her spiritual director dated 4 May 1943, Sr Lucia wrote that Our Lord "promises the end of the war shortly, in consideration of the act which His Holiness consented to carry out". (Antonio Martins, SJ, op. cit, p. 447). However, as the war drew to a close, the Red Army advanced across the countries of Eastern and Central Europe, and in its wake the Soviet Union installed a regime of Marxist atheism which bitterly persecuted the Church, as Our Lady had forewarned.

Meanwhile, on 4 May 1944 Pius XII instituted the feast of the Immaculate Heart of Mary, to be celebrated on 22 August.

The decree of institution stated that "the purpose of the feast is to obtain, through the help of the Blessed Mother of God, peace for all nations, freedom for the Church of Christ, conversion for sinners..." And in his next act approving the message of Fatima, Pius XII sent his legate, Cardinal Aloysius Masella, to crown the statue of Our Lady of Fatima on 13 May 1946, and proclaim her "Queen of Peace and of the World". That year was chosen because it was the tercentenary of Portugal's consecration to the Immaculate Conception by King John IV, in 1646. The crown was made from 1200 grammes of gold, melted down from wedding rings donated by the women of Portugal, and it contains 313 pearls and 2,679 precious stones.

1946 is also the year when the Bishops of Poland renewed the act that had been carried out in July 1920, when they had re-dedicated their nation to the Blessed Virgin, two years after Poland had recovered its independence and inaugurated the Second Republic. This second act was carried out on 8 September 1946 by the primate, Cardinal Hlond, together with the bishops and some 700,000 of the faithful, at the national shrine of Jasna Gora in Czestochowa, and the form that was used is significant because this time the consecration was made "to you and to your Immaculate Heart" - the exact words employed by Pius XII when he had first consecrated the world to the Immaculate Heart of Mary four years previously.

Was the future John Paul II present at this act, as a seminarian, less than two months before his ordination on 1

November? In view of Karol Wojtyla's devotion to Our Lady, it seems reasonable to reflect that even if he may not have been present in the vast crowd, in all probability the unprecedented character of the event itself, and the grave circumstances in which it took place, would have been foremost in his heart and thoughts, as well as those of a great many devout Catholics in Poland at that time. And may one attribute the astonishing preservation of the Church in Poland through the years of Marxist persecution that were to follow, to Our Lady's protection and intercession, in virtue of this act? There seems to be a distinct element of probability in that too, but this is not the place to enter into such a deep question.

However, we do know that, by this consecration, Poland became the first nation to follow the example of Portugal.

Our Lady of Fatima: Pilgrim Virgin

In 1947, there began the first of a series of international journeys by the Pilgrim Virgin statue of Our Lady. This story forms such a remarkable part of the whole Fatima apostolate, that we cannot omit to include this very brief summary.

The famous statue of Our Lady of Fatima which is still today venerated in the Little Chapel of the Apparitions, was carved by Thedim under the direction of Lucia, and enthroned on 13 June 1920. The statue first travelled out from the Sanctuary in April 1942, to a Catholic Youth Congress in Lisbon, and this caused such an upsurge of faith and conversions, that a second month-long journey to Lisbon and back was organised, for the tercentenary celebration of Portugal's consecration to the Immaculate Conception, on 8 December 1946. On the route to Lisbon, some white doves were released and spontaneously settled at Our Lady's feet, to remain there for days without food or drink. Then, at Mass in Lisbon, one of the doves perched on Our Lady's crown, turned to face the altar and remained with its wings outstretched while Communion was being given to some 3000 faithful. This event became known as "the miracle of the doves".

Since then this statue has made at least six further pilgrim journeys throughout the world, and it was in front of this venerable image, on the steps of St Peter's Basilica in Rome, that Pope John Paul II's consecrated the world to the Immaculate Heart of Mary, on 25th March 1984.

After the war had ended, at the proposal of a Belgian priest the statue first went on pilgrimage to an international Marian Congress at Maastricht in Holland, in September 1947. Thereafter, between 1947 and 1966, the first Pilgrim Virgin statue travelled ten times round the world, visiting some 3,700 parishes. An estimated 300 million people of different races and religions prayed before it, and Our Lady was received with particular enthusiasm by Moslems, Buddhists, Hindus and Sikhs. The image was present in Rome on 1 November 1950, the day when Pius XII solemnly defined the dogma of Our Lady's Assumption into Heaven. And on 13 October 1951, in his radio message to Fatima for the closing ceremonies of the extended Holy Year, the Pope commented in the following words on the image's world-wide travels:

"The miracles she performs along the way are such that we can scarcely believe what our eyes are seeing... under the maternal eye of the celestial Pilgrim there are no antagonisms of nationality or race or culture that divide... The Blessed Virgin... shows us the secure way to peace and the means to obtain it from Heaven..." (From *The Seers of Fatima*, Sept/Oct 1995, by permission of the editor, Fr L. Kondor, SVD).

In 1967, a number of Pilgrim Virgin statues were blessed by Pope Paul VI and delivered by the Blue Army to the national hierarchies of twenty-one countries, and four years later a further seventy statues were taken to individual nations.

One of the most celebrated journeys of the Pilgrim Virgin was the flight around the whole world in 1978, organised by the Blue Army of America.

The image received an overwhelming reception in South Korea, Taiwan and Singapore. Over one million people came out to greet Our Lady in Bombay, and President Sadat of Egypt and Prime Minister Begin of Israel granted it diplomatic immunity for the first civil airline flight direct from Cairo to Tel Aviv. In Rome, on 1st May some half a million people welcomed Our Lady, and through Secretary of State, Cardinal Villot, Pope Paul VI expressed "deep happiness over the solemn Marian ceremonies".

To Eastern Europe

At Warsaw, the Russian military locked the statue in the plane's cockpit, but this hostile gesture brought about a marvellous sequel. The Franciscans at Niepokolanow, St Maximilian Kolbe's 'City of Mary' just outside Warsaw, fashioned a wire outline of the statue, with the words "Our Mother never leaves Us!" Cardinal Wyszynski loaned a car, and the outline, which became a celebrity known as the "Absent Madonna", made a rapid visit to Cracow, Katowice and finally Czestochowa, where it was placed directly in front of the famous centuries-old Black Madonna.

The "Absent Madonna" was left in Poland, and so many copies were made that the Communist authorities, fearing the adverse publicity, asked for the real statue to be brought back! Cardinal Wyszynski agreed, on condition that he was permitted to build twenty-eight new churches. Before the statue returned to Poland in August 1979, it was blessed by the recently-elected Pope from Poland, John Paul II, at Castel Gandolfo. Then on 22 August, feast of the Queenship of Mary, the statue was placed on the altar of the first new church to be built in Warsaw under the Communists, alongside the wire outline they had left behind the previous year, and on the same day the government finally relented and gave permission for the first new seminary to be built in Warsaw.

Following the collapse of the former Soviet Union, the Pilgrim Virgin has visited Slovakia and Hungary, in 1994, and every diocese in Poland, for a whole year, ending in October

1996. On 8 December 1996, for the first time since Our Lady appeared in 1917 with a message concerning Russia, the statue was formally received in the Catholic Church of the Immaculate Conception in Moscow, and thereafter it spent three months in each of 'European' Russia, Siberia and Kazakhstan. As Fr Kondor reported in the Jan-March 1997 issue of *The Seers of Fatima*, during the Pilgrim Virgin's visit to Russia, her statue was received in Catholic, Orthodox and Protestant churches, and was frequently carried in procession by Orthodox priests.

The Blue Army 1947

Returning to the sequence of events in the reign of Pius XII, it was also in 1947 that a parish priest in America, Fr Harold Colgan, was led to found the Blue Army, as the World Apostolate of Fatima was originally called. He visited Fatima in May 1950, the idea of the Blue Army was welcomed by Bishop Jose Correia da Silva. At Rome, Fr Colgan was encouraged in his work by Pope Pius XII at a private audience on 8 May 1950. The Blue Army expanded rapidly, especially in America, and on 13 October 1956, its international head-quarters, *Domus Pacis* (House of Peace), was officially opened at Fatima by Cardinal Tisserant, Dean of the Sacred College of Cardinals, who acted as Pius XII's Legate for the occasion.

The World Apostolate of Fatima, the Blue Army, as it is now officially known, is a lay apostolate recognised by the Holy See, which works autonomously under the direction of the local hierarchy in some 140 countries. Its members pledge themselves to live and to bring others to live the message of Our Lady and her requests for prayer, penance and reparation for sin.

Pius XII sees miracle of the sun

Meanwhile, on 13 October 1951, Cardinal Tedeschini came to Fatima as the Pope's Legate, to preside over the closing of the Church's universal Holy Year. In his homily, the Cardinal spoke about the miracle of the sun in October 1917. Then, to the astonishment of the multitude of pilgrims, the Cardinal revealed that one year previously Pius XII himself had seen a repetition of the miracle of the sun in the Vatican gardens, at 4 o'clock in the afternoon, on 30 and 31 October, on 1 November, and once more, on the octave day of the Feast of All Saints. The miraculous repetition had taken place on and around the 1st November 1950 - the day on which the Pope had proclaimed the dogma of Mary's Assumption into Heaven, in his Apostolic Constitution, *Munificentissimus Deus*.

"The solar disc surrounded by its halo - who can gaze on it?" asked Cardinal Tedeschini. "He could, during those four days. Beneath the hand of Mary, he could observe the sun coming down, moving, convulsing, palpitating with life, transmitting, in a spectacle of celestial movements, silent but eloquent messages to the Vicar of Christ" (Quoted by Fr Antonio Martins, SJ, in *Fatima, Way of Peace*, p. 25).

Finally, Pius XII carried out two further acts signifying his approval of the message of Fatima. On 7 July 1952, the Pope consecrated the peoples of Russia to the Immaculate Heart of Mary; and on 12 November 1954, by the brief *Luce Superna*, Pius XII raised to the rank of Basilica the church of Our Lady of the Rosary at Fatima, which had been consecrated on 7 October 1953.

MESSAGE OF FATIMA:
JOHN XXIII AND PAUL VI

John XXIII was the first Pope to have visited Fatima, in May 1956, when he was Cardinal Patriarch of Venice, two and a half years before he was elected Pope, on 28 October 1958. In the first encyclical of his pontificate, *Ad Petri Cathedram*, issued on 29 June 1959, Pope John XXIII earnestly prayed God to grant unity and peace in the Church, "through the intercession of the Blessed Virgin Mary, Queen of Peace, to whose Immaculate Heart our predecessor, Pius XII consecrated the whole human race" (No. 65). Next, John XXIII opened the Second Vatican Council "under the auspices of the virgin Mother of God", as he said in his address, on 11 October 1962, the feast of the Divine Maternity of the Blessed Virgin Mary.

Pope institutes Fatima feast

Then, on 13 December 1962, in an important sign of papal recognition, John XXIII instituted the feast of Our Lady of the Rosary of Fatima. And on the first day the new feast was celebrated, 13 May 1963, Cardinal Larraona, the Pope's Legate at Fatima, and former Prefect of the Sacred Congregation of Rites, delivered a message to all the world's priests in which he stated that the message of Fatima "is a living realisation of the Gospel... Indeed, never has there been a supernatural manifestation of Our Lady of such rich spiritual content as that of Fatima, nor has any recognised apparition given us a message so clear, so maternal, so profound... Live and cause it to be lived".

There were several notable developments with regard to the message of Fatima in the pontificate of John XXIII's successor, Paul VI, who reigned from 21 June 1963 to 6 August 1978.

Paul VI and Vatican II

On 21 November 1964, at the end of its third session, the Second Vatican Council approved the Dogmatic Constitution on the Church, *Lumen Gentium*, whose final chapter 8 is entitled, "The Blessed Virgin Mary, Mother of God, in the mystery of Christ and the Church". Afterwards, Paul VI gave an address in the presence of all the Council Fathers, in the course of which the Pope highlighted the importance of this chapter, solemnly proclaimed that Mary is Mother of the Church, and made three separate references to Our Lady of Fatima.

"By the promulgation of today's constitution... it is the first time, in fact - and saying it fills our souls with profound emotion - that an Ecumenical Council has presented such a vast synthesis of the Catholic doctrine regarding the place which the Blessed Mary occupies in the mystery of Christ and of the Church...

The reality of the Church is not exhausted in its hierarchical structure, in its liturgy, in its sacraments, in its juridical ordinances. The intimate, the primary source of its sanctifying effectiveness is to be sought in its mystic union with Christ; a union which we cannot conceive as separate from her who is the Mother of the Word Incarnate and whom Jesus Christ Himself wanted closely united to Himself for our salvation. Thus the loving contemplation of the marvels worked by God in His Holy Mother must find its proper perspective in the vision of the Church. And knowledge of the true Catholic doctrine concerning the Blessed Virgin Mary will always be a key to the exact understanding of the mystery of Christ and of the Church ... Meditating on these close relationships between Mary and the Church... we have felt it opportune to consecrate in this very public session, a title which was suggested in honour of the Virgin from various parts of the Catholic world, and which is particularly dear to us because it sums up in an admirable synthesis the privileged position recognised by the Council for the Virgin in the Holy Church.

Therefore, for the glory of the Virgin Mary and for our own consolation, we proclaim the Most Blessed Mary Mother of the Church, that is to say, of all the people of God, of the faithful as well as of the pastors, who call her the most loving Mother. And we wish that the Mother of God should be honoured and invoked by the whole of Christendom through this most sweet title".

The Golden Rose

The Pope also considered it "particularly opportune" to recall Pius XII's consecration of the world to the Immaculate Heart of Mary; bearing that consecration in mind, he announced that he was sending a special mission to carry the Golden Rose to Fatima; and the Pope ended his address by proclaiming: "To your Immaculate Heart, O Mary, we finally commend the entire human race".

The Golden Rose was presented to the Sanctuary by Cardinal Cento on 13 May 1965, and carries the following inscription: "Pope Paul VI, imploring for the whole Church the patronage of the Mother of God, offers the Golden Rose to the Sanctuary of Fatima, 13 May 1965".

It is not known exactly when the custom of presenting the Golden Rose began, but apparently it was already ancient in the time of Pope St Leo IX, who reigned from 1049 to 1055. Traditionally it is given to notable churches and sanctuaries as a special mark of esteem, and blessed by the Pope on Laetare Sunday, the fourth Sunday in Lent, when the Church bids her children look forward with joy to Easter (laetare means: rejoice), and our redemption from sin by the risen Christ. The golden flower symbolises the kingship of Christ, the fragrance of the rose, His sweet odour; and the thorns and red tint speak of His Passion.

Paul VI goes to Fatima

On Saturday 13th May 1967, the vigil of Pentecost, Paul VI became the first Pope to travel on pilgrimage to Fatima, in a visit which was private in character and lasted only one day, as the Pope flew back to Rome the same evening. In his General Audience of 3rd May, Paul VI said that "the spiritual reason, which gives to this journey its proper significance, is to pray once more, and with greater humility and devotion, for Peace".

On 12th May, Paul VI's Legate, Cardinal Costa Nunes, arrived in Fatima, and his letter of appointment from the Pope was read out. In it, Paul VI wrote: "Let all then, in such grave circumstances, love and venerate the Immaculate Heart of the Blessed Virgin Mary, fountain of goodness, mercy and grace, let them endeavour to hasten her indubitable triumph". Then, in his homily at Mass on 13th, the Pope said:

"So great is our desire to honour the holy Virgin Mary, Mother of Christ and therefore Mother of God and our Mother, so great is our confidence... so great is our need of her intercession with Christ, her Divine Son... that we have come as a humble and trusting pilgrim to this blessed Sanctuary, where the 50th anniversary of the apparitions of Fatima is being celebrated today, and where the 25th anniversary of the consecration of the world to the Immaculate Heart of Mary is being commemorated... The first intention (of the pilgrimage) is for the Church... for its internal peace... We want to ask of Mary a living Church, a true Church, a united Church, a Holy Church

... The second intention of our pilgrimage fills our hearts: the world, peace in the world!... (the world) is full of tremendously deadly armaments, and it has not progressed morally as much as it has scientifically and technically... therefore, we say: the world is in danger. For this reason we have come to the feet of the Queen of Peace to ask for the gift, which only God can give, of peace. Yes, peace, a gift of God which supposes His intervention, Divine, good, merciful and mysterious".

In his apostolic exhortation, *Signum Magnum*, issued on the same day, Paul VI recalled Pius XII's consecration of 1942, and urged "all members of the Church to consecrate themselves once again to the Immaculate Heart of Mary, to translate this pious act into their daily lives. In this way they will comply ever more closely with God's will, and as imitators of their heavenly Queen, they will be truly recognised as her offspring".

The presence of the Vicar of Christ at the exact place where Our Lady had appeared to the three little shepherds fifty years previously, constituted the highest approval that had yet been accorded to the message of Fatima by the papacy. It was fitting, therefore, that after Mass on the altar in front of the Basilica, the Pope greeted Sr Lucia, the seer chosen by heaven to receive Our Lady's message, and with a simple gesture, presented her to the vast crowd of pilgrims below. Bishop Joao Venancio, the second Bishop of the restored diocese of Leiria-Fatima, later stated that this gesture of the Pope indicated: what Lucia stands for, I stand behind.

It was also appropriate that in the Basilica, not far from where the Pope was standing, lay the mortal remains of Lucia's cousins, Jacinta and Francisco; they had been translated to the Basilica in 1951 and 1952 respectively, and placed in a simple tomb in each transept, with Our Lady and the three Popes looking down on them from the painting above the High Altar. It was appropriate that Paul VI met Lucia near their tombs, because in the course of the apparitions, it emerged that little Jacinta, the youngest of the three children and aged only 7 at the time of the apparitions, had a special vocation to pray and offer sacrifices to God for the Pope, while Lucia's mission was to convey Our Lady's message to the Church, and Francisco was called to console the hidden Jesus with his prayers.

One day, some priests asked the children to pray for the Holy Father. Having learned who the Holy Father was, Jacinta conceived such love for him that when she made her sacrifice offering, "O my Jesus, it is for love of You ..", she added, "and for the Holy Father", and she always said three Hail Marys for the Holy Father, at the end of the Rosary. Later, Jacinta was favoured with two remarkable visions of the Holy Father. In the first, "I don't know how it was, but I saw the Holy Father in a very big house, kneeling by a table with his head buried in his hands, and he was weeping. Some were throwing stones, others were cursing him and using bad language. Poor Holy Father, we must pray very much for him". On another occasion, she called out to Lucia, "can't you see all those highways and roads and fields full of people, who are crying with hunger and have nothing to eat? And the Holy Father in a church, praying before the Immaculate Heart of Mary, and so many people praying with him?"

Finally, Lucia tells us that sometimes Jacinta would say: "How I would love to see the Holy Father! So many people come here, but the Holy Father never does!" This wish, first granted in the reign of Paul VI, was to be fulfilled again in a more complete manner by his successor, Pope John Paul II. On 13 May 1982, after the Adeus procession, the Pope wished to visit the basilica. He prayed first at the tomb of Francisco, then crossed to pray at the tomb of Jacinta. On arising, he met Sr Lucia, who must have experienced great joy at being able to pray with the Pope on her first visit to the tomb of her closest childhood friend, under the gaze of Our Lady.

Francisco and Jacinta saints?

On 13 May 1989, John Paul II promulgated the decree of the heroic virtues of the Servants of God, Francisco and Jacinta Marto, granting them the title Venerable. The next step in the process of their canonisation will come when the Church declares that a miracle has been obtained through their intercession. Fr L. Kondor, SVD, is Vice-Postulator for the Causes of Canonisation of Francisco and Jacinta, and in the September 1997 issue of his quarterly bulletin, *The Seers of Fatima*, he reported that a decision is now awaited from the Sacred Congregation for the Causes of the Saints, about a cure attributed to the intercession of Francisco and Jacinta in the diocese of Leiria-Fatima, the canonical process for which was delivered to Rome on 23rd June 1997.

JOHN PAUL II CONSECRATES RUSSIA, 1984

It is the unanimous judgment of the Holy See, the Bishop of Leiria-Fatima, leading Portuguese experts, and Sr Lucia, that by his act of consecration on 25 March 1984, Pope John Paul II has fulfilled the request of Our Lady for the consecration of Russia. 'Is Russia now consecrated?' Sr Lucia was asked by the Apostolic Nuncio, who visited her after the Pope had carried out the act. 'Yes, now it is', I answered. The Nuncio then said: 'Now we wait for the miracle'. I answered, 'God will keep his word'" (cited in *Fatima, Russia & Pope John Paul II*, p. 25).

John Paul II's pilgrimage to Fatima

John Paul II went on pilgrimage to Fatima in 1982 because, as he said in his homily on 13th May, "on this very day last year, in St Peter's Square in Rome, the attempt on the Pope's life was made, in mysterious coincidence with the anniversary of the first apparition at Fatima". On the previous evening, the Pope said that after the attempt on his life "my thoughts turned immediately to this Sanctuary to place in the heart of the heavenly Mother my thanks for having saved me from danger .. And in the coincidence - there are no mere coincidences in the plans of Divine Providence - I saw also an appeal and, who knows, a reminder of the message which came from here".

No doubt, therefore, it was Our Lady's presence at a moment of extreme mortal danger, that led the Pope to make a deep study of the documents related to Fatima at an opportune moment, while he was convalescing. "I brought them to him", stated Bishop Hnilica in an interview published in the March 1990 issue of *30 Days*. "Some of the texts were originals. He read everything with extreme attention".

Acts of Consecration, 1982 and 1984

When the Pope went to Fatima, he not only thanked Our Lady for saving his life. Fully briefed on the message, for the first time in the history of Fatima the Pope delivered a homily with profound teaching that explained both the message in general, and in particular, the act of consecration to Mary's Immaculate Heart, which he carried out on that occasion for the first time.

However, since not all the world's bishops had received the Pope's letter in time to join in his act of consecration, John Paul II accepted that it would have to be repeated, to be fully collegial. Hence a second consecration was carried out on 25 March 1984, on the steps of St Peter's Basilica in Rome, near to where he had suffered the attempt on his life almost three years before, and in front of the image of Our Lady, which had been specially flown over from the Chapel of the Apparitions at Fatima.

Mikhail Gorbachev

In the same month that the Pope effected the consecration of Russia, Mikhail Gorbachev was promoted as head of the Foreign Affairs Committee of the Soviet Union, and almost exactly one year later, he became General Secretary of the Communist Party, after the death of Konstantin Chernenko on 11 March 1985.

As soon as he came to power, Mr Gorbachev announced his programme of perestroika (restructuring) and glasnost (openness), in 1986 he outlined its principles to the Communist Party Congress, and in 1987 he began the process of political democratisation. In the same year a thaw became apparent in Soviet attitudes towards religion, while in Rome the Pope designated the period from the eve of Pentecost 1987 to the feast of the Assumption on 15 August 1988 as a Marian Year in preparation for the jubilee of the year 2000. In a spectacular television link-up, the Pope opened the Marian Year from the Basilica of St Mary Major in Rome, praying the Rosary for world peace in union with tens of thousands of the faithful gathered in sixteen of the major shrines to Our Lady throughout the world.

In 1988, Mr Gorbachev was appointed President of the Soviet Union, and when in November 1989, popular uprisings began against the Communist governments of Eastern Europe, and the Warsaw Pact was dissolved, President Gorbachev refused to intervene to repress the new democratic forces that had been unleashed by his programme of perestroika and glasnost. In December of the same year, President Gorbachev had an unprecedented meeting with Pope John Paul II at the Vatican, following which, he revealed later, they had kept up an intense exchange of letters.

The final end of the USSR, after a process of auto-dissolution, effectively came on Christmas Day 1991, when President Gorbachev went on television to announce his resignation as President. In a remarkable address to the nation, he stated: "When I found myself at the helm of this state, it was already clear that... we had to change everything radically... I am convinced that the democratic reform we launched in the spring of 1985 was historically correct. This society has acquired freedom... the totalitarian system has been eliminated... Human rights are being treated as the supreme principle".

John Paul II and Gorbachev

Even more remarkable, perhaps, is the article published by Mr Gorbachev a few weeks later in the Turin daily, *La Stampa*, on 3 March 1992, in which he disclosed the understanding that had developed between himself and the Pope, through their intense exchange of letters. "I don't have the slightest difficulty in admitting that I was in accord with many ideas in his discourses", wrote the former President; "...everything that happened in Eastern Europe during these last few years would not have been possible without the presence of this Pope".

At Mr Gorbachev's request, his publishers personally delivered his article to John Paul II and then, following an audience which they had been granted, in their issue of 4 March, the next day, *La Stampa* published the Pope's comments on the article.

The Pope said that Gorbachev's words were sincere, because he was a man of integrity, and... "it's true, there was something instinctive between us, as if we had already known each other. And I know why that was: our meeting had been prepared by Providence... He does not profess to be a believer, but with me I recall he spoke of the great importance of prayer and of the inner side of man's life. I truly believe our meeting was prepared by Providence" (*La Stampa*, 4 March 1992).

Ten years earlier, referring to the attempt on his life, John Paul II had said "there are no mere coincidences in the plans of Divine Providence". Returning to Rome from his second pilgrimage to Fatima, on 15 May 1991, he observed: "I consider this entire decade to be a free gift, given to me in a special way by Divine Providence".

Eastern Europe and Fatima

Meanwhile, in May 1990, Cardinal Meisner of Cologne, who until two years previously had been Bishop of Berlin in East Germany, came with the first pilgrimage to Fatima since the Second World War from one of the recently-liberated Eastern bloc countries. In his homily, Cardinal Meisner thanked Mary "in the name of Christians from this region of Europe, ... who, going out from Fatima, took under her special protection all of Eastern Europe, which was formerly so Christian".

Commenting on the Cardinal's words, the Bishop of Leiria-Fatima, stated: "It is lawful to think that everything which surprisingly has happened in Eastern and Central Europe - religious liberty recognised by governments, institution of the sacred hierarchy, respect for the fundamental rights of the human person - can be attributed to the intervention of Our Lady, solicitous Mother of all men and all peoples".

Then in July 1990, Cardinal Paskai, Primate of Hungary, came with another important pilgrimage, to show their gratitude for Mary's intercession. "Profound changes have begun in the countries of Central and Eastern Europe (which)... cannot be explained by purely human factors. Politicians who are believers also acknowledge that the hand of God can be seen in these changes... I wish to manifest here, in the Sanctuary of Fatima, my deepest conviction that we are experiencing the intervention of the Most Holy Virgin" (Fr L. Kondor, SVD, *Seers of Fatima*, May-August 1990).

In the following year, John Paul II returned to Fatima in May, on the tenth anniversary of the attempt on his life, and in his Act of Entrustment thanked Our Lady "because you have always listened to us. You showed yourself a mother... Mother of the nations by the unexpected changes which restored confidence to peoples who were oppressed and humiliated for so long... my Mother for ever, and especially on 13 May 1981, when I felt your helpful presence at my side..."

1992 Diamond Jubilee

For the opening celebrations of the Diamond Jubilee year of Our Lady's apparitions in 1992, the Pope sent to Fatima as his Legate his Secretary of State, Cardinal Sodano. In the course of his homily on 13 May, Cardinal Sodano stated: "This convinced and insistent invocation of the protection of Mary, Queen of Peace, of which the Supreme Pontiffs have made themselves the sounding-trumpet, has found a clamorous historic response in the extraordinary facts of reconciliation and of political and religious liberty, verified in Europe and in many parts of the world, in these latter times. These changes on the international scene led the Supreme Pontiff John Paul II to return to Fatima, to raise a solemn and public act of thanksgiving to the Lord of History for the marvels realised in the world, through Mary's intercession". On the same occasion, Cardinal Jan Korec came from Nitra in Slovakia and gave a moving testimony at the Congress on "Fatima and Peace", in which he stated: "The persecution lasted for forty years in our country and was very, very hard. But we always had confidence in the Mother of God, the Virgin of Fatima".

It is true that in Lithuania, Poland and Hungary, former Communists subsequently swept back into power. But, as the

Pope explained in an interview published in *La Stampa* on 2 November 1993, this signified "not so much a return of the Communists as such, but rather a reaction to the inefficiency of the new governments... which is not at all surprising. The only political class that existed for fifty years was that of the Communists". After the elections in Hungary in May 1994, when the Socialists won back 54% of the seats, having been reduced to 8% in 1990, Cardinal Paskai commented: "Communism is a definitive failure, both ideologically and economically... the democratic process is irreversible. All the Socialists might do is to modify it on the basis of their own platform" (*30 Days*, No. 6, 1994, pp. 22-23).

Evangelisation

Clearly many grave questions remain to be resolved in the countries of the former Soviet Union, and there are bound to be reverses and failures, because the transition between two systems so diametrically opposed is inevitably very difficult. Despite that, there is one transcending gain which has not been reversed and which may be attributed to the intervention of Our Lady: namely, the complete cessation of the Marxist campaign against religion. Consequently, the Church is now free to pursue her evangelical mission, and faces the enormous challenge of bringing back to God a society that has been almost completely severed from its moral and spiritual roots by decades of atheistic indoctrination and persecution.

John Paul II's Teaching on Fatima

Interpretation of Fatima by the Church

On his first pilgrimage to Fatima in 1982, John Paul II delivered a homily during the Mass of 13 May which is of particular importance because by this pronouncement, for the first time since Our Lady's apparitions in 1917, the Pope, guided by the Holy Spirit, issued a substantial body of teaching on the message of Fatima.

As Fr Messias Coelho, SJ, a leading Portuguese authority on Fatima, has explained, "the apparitions and their messages are charisms, that is, acts of the Holy Spirit". Hence, "their interpretation - to be correct - also has to be an act of the Holy Spirit. He is the Soul of the Church. So, the only correct interpretation is that of the Church and not that of seers. Usually the charism of seers consists only in telling the Church what they saw and heard" (*Mensagem de Fatima*, 30 August 1989).

One must also bear in mind that "it is the Pope who holds the supreme authority to judge on the message which any apparition, even when true, brings to the Church and to the world" (cited in *Fatima the Great Sign*, p. 90) - to quote Dr Joaquin Alonso, CMF, an outstanding Marian theologian, and the first person appointed to work on the official history of Fatima, up to his death in 1981.

Accordingly, in his homily John Paul II has given the Church teaching which will enable us to understand and accept what is God's will for us in the message of Fatima at this important moment in salvation history, when the Church faces new challenges of opportunity and hope, but also new forms of resistance and rejection, as it prepares to enter the third millennium.

What, then, is the status of the message of Fatima according to the teaching of the Church? Particular teaching has been issued by Pope John Paul II and the Bishops of Leiria-Fatima. In general, one may say that, "so far as the heart of the message of Fatima goes - prayer, penance, reparation and the compassionate Immaculate Heart of Mary - the Church's approval is absolute", as Fr Eaman Carroll, O. Carm, the noted Mariologist, stated at a symposium on the message of Fatima at Marymount University, America, in July 1989. "No Catholic is free to reject these key aspects of Christian belief and practice. The Church's judgment here is infallible because these are matters that affect the very core of our Christian and Catholic lives. As far as the particular circumstances that gave rise to the Fatima message are concerned, the Church has warmly recommended acceptance of the apparitions, but only as a matter of human faith... This may seem strange, but we cannot make obligations where the Church does not command us. It is important that we do not impose on others the obligation to accept private revelations" (quoted in *Exploring Fatima*, AMI Press, USA, 1989, p. 12).

John Paul II's homily, 1982

John Paul II explained the Church's acceptance of the message of Fatima, in the following three paragraphs taken from his homily of 13 May 1982: "The Church has always taught and continues to proclaim that God's revelation was brought to completion in Jesus Christ, who is the fullness of that revelation, and that 'no new public revelation is to be expected before the glorious manifestation of Our Lord' (*Dei Verbum*, 4). The Church evaluates and judges private revelations by the criterion of conformity with that single public Revelation.

If the Church has accepted the message of Fatima, it is above all because that message contains a truth and a call whose basic content is the truth and the call of the Gospel itself. 'Repent and believe in the Gospel' (Mk 1:15). These are the first words that the Messiah addressed to humanity. The message of Fatima is, in its basic nucleus, a call to conversion and repentance, as in the Gospel. This call was uttered at the beginning of the twentieth century, and it was thus addressed particularly to this present century. The Lady of the message seems to have read with special insight the 'signs of the times', the signs of our time... The appeal of the Lady of the message of Fatima is so deeply rooted in the Gospel and the whole of Tradition that the Church feels that the message imposes a commitment on her.

She has responded through the Servant of God, Pius XII, (whose episcopal ordination took place precisely on 13 May 1917). He consecrated the human race and especially the peoples of Russia to the Immaculate Heart of Mary".

Importance of Fatima

Fifteen years after delivering this homily, the Pope showed the continuing importance he attaches to the message of Fatima, when he stated, in a message to the Bishop of Leiria - Fatima dated 1 October 1997:

"On the threshold of the third millennium, as we observe the signs of the times in this 20th century, Fatima is certainly one of the greatest, among other reasons because its message announces many of the later events and conditions them on the response to its appeals: signs such as the two world wars, but also great gatherings of nations and peoples marked by dialogue and peace; the oppression and turmoil suffered by various nations and peoples, but also the voice and the opportunities given to peoples and individuals who in the meantime have emerged on the international scene; the crises, desertions and many sufferings of the Church's members, but also a renewed and intense feeling of solidarity and mutual dependence in Christ's Mystical Body, which is being strengthened in all the baptised, in accordance with their vocation and mission; the separation from and abandonment of God by individuals and societies, but also the in-breaking of the Spirit of Truth in hearts and communities to the point of sacrifice and martyrdom to save 'God's image and likeness in man' (cf. Gn 1:27), to save man from himself. Among these and other signs of the times, as I said, Fatima stands out and helps us see the hand of God, our providential Guide and patient and compassionate Father also in the 20th century" (*Osservatore Romano*, 29 Oct. 1997).

John Paul II's teaching on Fatima

The Pope's homily of 13 May 1982 needs to be read, prayed and meditated in order to grasp the full extent of its meaning. It is printed in full, as Appendix III, in my earlier book, *Fatima, Russia and Pope John Paul II*. The most important themes it contains are as follows: The Pope opened his homily by commenting on Jn 19:27, the concluding words of the Gospel of the day. "... The Mother of God became the Mother of man. From that hour, John 'took her to his own home'... and became by Christ's will the son of the Mother of God. And in John every human being became her child... Mary's motherhood in our regard is manifested in... the Marian sanctuaries... (where) that unique testament of the Crucified Lord is wonderfully actualised... in them man 'takes her into his own home'".

"In the light of the mystery of Mary's spiritual motherhood", says John Paul II, "let us seek to understand the extraordinary message, which began on 13 May 1917 to resound throughout the world from Fatima".

Man's rejection of God

As we have seen above, the Pope taught that the basic nucleus of the message of Fatima is "a call to conversion and repentance, as in the Gospel... The call to repentance is a motherly one... In the light of a mother's love, we understand the whole message of the Lady of Fatima. The greatest obstacle to man's journey towards God is sin, perseverance in sin, and finally, denial of God. The deliberate blotting out of God from the world of human thought. The detachment from Him of the whole of man's earthly activity. The rejection of God by man... Can the Mother who, with all the force of the love that she fosters in the Holy Spirit, desires everyone's salvation, keep silence on what undermines the very bases of their salvation? No, she cannot.

And so, while the message of Our Lady of Fatima is a motherly one, it is also strong and decisive... It invites to repentance, it gives a warning, it calls to prayer, it recommends the Rosary. The message is addressed to every human being. The love of the Saviour's Mother reaches every place touched by the work of salvation. Her care extends to every individual of our time, and to all the societies, nations and peoples. Societies menaced by apostasy, threatened by moral degradation. The collapse of morality involves the collapse of societies..."

The latter part of the above paragraph echoes the following comment by the Fathers of the Second Vatican Council on the role of the Blessed Virgin in the life of the Church, in Chapter 8 of *Lumen Gentium* (No. 62), where they state: "Her motherly love makes her care for her Son's brethren still on their pilgrimage, still involved in dangers and difficulties until they be brought to the happiness of their fatherland".

"Consecrating ourselves to Mary", the Pope continued in his homily, "means accepting her help to offer ourselves and the whole of mankind to Him who is holy, infinitely holy... by having recourse to her motherly heart, which beneath the Cross was opened to love for every human being... Consecrating the world to the Immaculate Heart of the Mother means returning beneath the Cross of the Son. It means consecrating this world to the pierced heart of the Saviour, bringing it back to the very source of its redemption. My heart is oppressed when I see the sin of the world and the whole range of menaces gathering like a dark cloud over mankind, but it also rejoices with hope as I once more do what has been done by my predecessors when they consecrated the world to the Heart of the Mother ...Doing this means consecrating the world to Him who is infinite Holiness. This holiness means redemption. It means a love more powerful than evil. No 'sin of the world' can ever overcome this Love. Once more this act is being done. Mary's appeal is not just for once. Her appeal must be taken up by generation after generation, in accordance with the ever new 'signs of the times'. It must be unceasingly returned to. It must ever be taken up anew".

In Chapter 8 of *Lumen Gentium*, (No. 69), we find a similar appeal: "All Christ's faithful must issue urgent pleas to the Mother of God and Mother of men... Now that she is placed high in heaven above all the blessed and the angels, they must plead with her to make intercession before her Son ..".

Conversion from sin

As we have seen, in this homily the Pope teaches that the Mother of man who desires everyone's salvation, intervened at Fatima because she cannot "keep silence on what undermines the very bases of their salvation", namely: sin, which has "made itself firmly at home in the world, and denial of God, which has become widespread in the ideologies, ideas and plans of human beings".

The Pope summarised this teaching in the General Audience on his return to Rome from Fatima in May 1982: "The threat on the part of the forces of evil comes particularly from the errors that have been spread in this very century of ours, errors based on the denial of God and the attempt to cut off mankind completely from him, positing human life without God and even against God. In the very heart of the message that came from Fatima at the beginning of our century, we find a powerful warning about these errors" (*Osservatore Romano*, 24 May 1982).

It is particularly important to take note of this aspect of the Pope's teaching, since in it, for the first time in the history of Fatima, the Pope, guided by the Holy Spirit, has defined with admirable precision the nature of the errors at the heart of Our Lady's warning. He said they consist in the "denial of God. The deliberate blotting out of God from the world of human thought, the detachment from Him of the whole of man's earthly activity. The rejection of God by man".

The Denial of God

This definition has established a new criterion on which to base our understanding and response to the message of Fatima. Knowing that this interpretation is totally secure, since it comes from the Pope, guided by the Holy Spirit, we can now clearly understand what Our Lady was referring to, when she spoke of "the errors of Russia".

Firstly, in defining precisely what those errors are, John Paul II's teaching also makes clear what they do not consist of, and thereby delivers us from mistaken interpretations and consequent misunderstandings from which the message of Fatima has suffered and in some respects continues to suffer.

Secondly, in the light of this teaching we understand why the message of Fatima "speaks ever more urgently to the men and women of today", as Cardinal Ratzinger stated at Fatima in October 1996.

It is evident that John Paul II's definition covers a wide spectrum - all those "ideologies, ideas and plans of human beings" in modern society, in fact, into which the spirit of "the rejection of God by man" has entered. In a number of his subsequent Encyclicals and other important pronouncements, John Paul II has been teaching that it is precisely the same universal error of the denial and rejection of God which lies at the root of various grave disorders afflicting society today. As the Pope warned at Fatima in 1991, in his Act of Entrustment, Marxism has been replaced by another form of atheism which "praising freedom, tends to destroy the roots of human and Christian morality". This particular aspect of the Pope's teaching on the message of Fatima has acquired new and urgent relevance to the situation of the Church today.

In his Encyclical on the Holy Spirit, *Dominum et Vivificantem*, issued on 18 May 1986, the Pope wrote that materialism is the clearest form of resistance to the Holy Spirit because it is "systematically atheistic" (Nos. 56, 57). Religious indifference and atheism in its "most widespread form of secularism" were ever-increasing, he said, in *Christifideles Laici* (No. 4), issued on 30 December 1988. The effect of atheism in modern society, he wrote in the Encyclical *Centesimus Annus*, issued on 1 May 1991, was that it "deprives the person of his foundation" (No. 13).

In broader terms, the Pope summarised the same theme as the inheritance of sin which "shows itself as an insane aspiration to build the world - a world created by humanity - as if God did not exist. And also as if there were no cross on Golgotha" (*Homily at Fatima*, 13 May 1991). In the following year, he went on to show that it is the family which "is placed at the centre of the great struggle between good and evil" (*Letter to Families*, February 1992, pp. 29, 68), and in May 1993, the Pope told some American Bishops that the first step had to be "re-establishing an adequate sense of sin ...to confront the grave spiritual crisis .. of an 'eclipse of conscience'" (*Agenda for the Third Millennium*, p. 150).

In his book, *Crossing the Threshold of Hope*, published in November 1994, the Pope said that Western thought had been largely dominated by the struggle against God for three centuries. "Marxist collectivism is nothing more than a 'cheap version' of this plan. Today a similar plan is revealing itself in all its danger and, at the same time, in all its faultiness" (p. 132).

Finally, in his Encyclical *Evangelium Vitae*, on the Gospel of Life, issued in March 1995, the Pope wrote (No. 21): "In seeking the deepest roots of the struggle between the 'culture of life' and the 'culture of death'... we have to go to the heart of the tragedy being experienced by modern man: the eclipse of the sense of God and of man... at the heart of the moral conscience... with all its various and deadly consequences for life (No. 24)... We are all involved... with the inescapable responsibility of choosing to be unconditionally pro-life (No. 28)... The one who accepted 'Life' in the name of all and for the sake of all was Mary, the Virgin Mother; she is thus most closely and personally associated with the Gospel of life" (No. 102).

It is evident that God has caused the papacy and the Fatima message to radiate with a special new lustre in the pontificate of John Paul II - beginning with the drama on 13 May 1981, when the Pope experienced Our Lady's helpful presence at his side, then through his response to Our Lady's message by his profound teaching and his acts of consecration, and finally by his personal example in living the message through the "higher Gospel of suffering", as he said after breaking his hip on 29 April 1994.

In the Holy Father's most recent message to the Bishop of Leiria-Fatima, dated 1 October 1997, on the occasion, as he noted, of the 80th anniversary of the miraculous 'dance of the sun', the Pope stated: "On the threshold of the third millennium, as we observe the signs of the times in this 20th century, Fatima is certainly one of the greatest, among other reasons because its message announces many of the later events and conditions them on the response to its appeals .."

In the view of this writer, the teaching and acts of Pope John Paul II themselves constitute further 'signs of the times' through which, at a particularly significant moment in salvation history, God has clearly expressed His continuing approval of the message of Fatima.

Among the most notable of these signs was the remarkable collapse, peacefully from within, of the Marxist atheist persecution of the Church in Central and Eastern Europe, following the Pope's act of consecration on 25 March 1984.

JOHN PAUL II'S TEACHING ON FATIMA 85

Thereby, one may reflect, did not God in a certain sense demonstrate that the prevailing spirit of the rejection and denial of God, about which the Pope continues to warn the Church, will likewise be overcome through the intercession of the Immaculate Heart of Mary? And was it not also a sign, that this will come to pass when the Church, following the teaching and example of her Chief Shepherd, accepts and responds to the Mother's message, especially her request for daily recitation of the Rosary and for the Five First Saturdays Communion of Reparation - the counterpart, that is now awaited from the Church, of the act of consecration that had been awaited from the Pope?

THE WORLD APOSTOLATE OF FATIMA

The World Apostolate of Fatima, a lay apostolate approved by the Bishops' Conference of England and Wales in 1982, promotes the requests of the Blessed Virgin at Fatima for personal conversion, daily Rosary for World peace, the offerings of prayers, sacrifices and one's daily duty for sinners, and especially, the Five Saturdays devotion of Eucharistic reparation for sin.

For Full details of membership, without cost or obligation, please send 9" x 4" SAE (20p) to:

George Donovan,
President, World Apostolate of Fatima,
36 Bowood Road,
SWINDON
Wilts SN1 4LP

Informative Catholic Reading

We hope that you have enjoyed reading this booklet.

If you would like to find out more about CTS booklets - we'll send you our free information pack and catalogue.

Please send us your details:

Name ....

Address ....

....

....

Postcode ....

Telephone..

Email ....

Send to: CTS, 40-46 Harleyford Road,
          Vauxhall, London
          SE11 5AY

Tel: 020 7640 0042
Fax: 020 7640 0046
Email: info@cts-online.org.uk

Bring the riches of the faith to your parish community

Add a CTS dimension to your parish with our new bookstands
- Wall-mountable unit
- Free-standing unit
- Two-tier unit (wall-mountable or table-top)

Please send me information on CTS display units and the half price offer on books.

SPECIAL OFFER
Get 50% off CTS booklets when you order a display unit*

Name ....
Address ....
....
....
Postcode ....
Telephone..
Email ....

Send to: CTS, 40-46 Harleyford Road,
          Vauxhall, London
          SE11 5AY

Tel: 020 7640 0042 Fax: 020 7640 0046
Email: info@cts-online.org.uk

* terms & conditions apply. Details on request